Smith

D1425177

by Iain Gray

Lang**Syne**

PUBLISHING

WRITING *to* REMEMBER

LangSyne

PUBLISHING

WRITING *to* REMEMBER

Vineyard Business Centre,
Pathhead, Midlothian EH37 5XP
Tel: 01875 321 203 Fax: 01875 321 233
E-mail: info@lang-syne.co.uk
www.langsyneshop.co.uk

Design by Roy Boyd
Printed by Montgomery Litho, Glasgow
© Lang Syne Publishers Ltd 2010

ISBN 978-1-85217-118-6

Smith

*Echoes of a far distant past
can still be found in most names*

Chapter one:

Origins of Scottish surnames

by George Forbes

It all began with the Normans.

For it was they who introduced surnames into common usage more than a thousand years ago, initially based on the title of their estates, local villages and chateaux in France to distinguish and identify these landholdings, usually acquired at the point of a bloodstained sword.

Such grand descriptions also helped enhance the prestige of these arrogant warlords and generally glorify their lofty positions high above the humble serfs slaving away below in the pecking order who only had single names, often with Biblical connotations as in Pierre and Jacques.

The only descriptive distinctions

among this peasantry concerned their occupations, like Pierre the swineherd or Jacques the ferryman.

The Normans themselves were originally Vikings (or Northmen) who raided, colonised and eventually settled down around the French coastline.

They had sailed up the Seine in their longboats in 900AD under their ferocious leader Rollo and ruled the roost in north east France before sailing over to conquer England, bringing their relatively new tradition of having surnames with them.

It took another hundred years for the Normans to percolate northwards and surnames did not begin to appear in Scotland until the thirteenth century.

These adventurous knights brought an aura of chivalry with them and it was said no damsel of any distinction would marry a man unless he had at least two names.

The family names included that of Scotland's great hero Robert De Brus and his compatriots were warriors from families like the De Morevils, De Umphravils, De Berkelais, De Quincis, De Viponts and De Vaux.

As the knights settled the boundaries of their vast estates, they took territorial names, as in Hamilton, Moray, Crawford, Cunningham, Dunbar, Ross, Wemyss, Dundas, Galloway, Renfrew, Greenhill, Hazelwood, Sandylands and Church-hill.

Other names, though not with any obvious geographical or topographical features, nevertheless derived from ancient parishes like Douglas, Forbes, Dalyell and Guthrie.

Other surnames were coined in connection with occupations, castles or legendary deeds. Stuart originated in the word steward, a prestigious post which was an integral part of any large medieval household. The same applied to Cooks, Chamberlains, Constables and Porters.

Borders towns and forts - needed in

areas like the Debateable Lands which were constantly fought over by feuding local families - had their own distinctive names; and it was often from them that the resident groups took their communal titles, as in the Grahams of Annandale, the Elliots and Armstrongs of the East Marches, the Scotts and Kerrs of Teviotdale and Eskdale.

Even physical attributes crept into surnames, as in Small, Little and More (the latter being 'beg' in Gaelic), Long or Lang, Stark, Stout, Strong or Strang and even Jolly.

Mieklejohns would have had the strength of several men, while Littlejohn was named after the legendary sidekick of Robin Hood.

Colours got into the act with Black, White, Grey, Brown and Green (Red developed into Reid, Ruddy or Ruddiman). Blue was rare and nobody ever wanted to be associated with yellow.

Pompous worthies took the name Wiseman, Goodman and Goodall.

Words intimating the sons of leading figures were soon affiliated into the language as in Johnson, Adamson, Richardson and Thomson, while the Norman equivalent of Fitz (from the French-Latin 'filius' meaning 'son') cropped up in Fitzmaurice and Fitzgerald.

The prefix 'Mac' was 'son of' in Gaelic and clans often originated with occupations - as in MacNab being sons of the Abbot, MacPherson and MacVicar being sons of the minister and MacIntosh being sons of the chief.

The church's influence could be found in the names Kirk, Clerk, Clarke, Bishop, Friar and Monk. Proctor came from a church official, Singer and Sangster from choristers, Gilchrist and Gillies from Christ's servant, Mitchell, Gilmory and Gilmour from servants of St Michael and Mary, Malcolm from a servant of Columba and Gillespie from a bishop's servant.

The rudimentary medical profession was represented by Barber (a trade which also once included dentistry and surgery) as well as Leech or Leitch.

Businessmen produced Merchants, Mercers, Monypennies, Chapmans, Sellers and Scales, while down at the old village watermill the names that cropped up included Miller, Walker and Fuller.

Other self explanatory trades included Coopers, Brands, Barkers, Tanners, Skinners, Brewsters and Brewers, Tailors, Saddlers, Wrights, Cartwrights, Smiths, Harpers, Joiners, Sawyers, Masons and Plumbers.

Even the scenery was utilised as in Craig, Moor, Hill, Glen, Wood and Forrest.

Rank, whether high or low, took its place with Laird, Barron, Knight, Tennant, Farmer, Husband, Granger, Grieve, Shepherd, Shearer and Fletcher.

The hunt and the chase supplied Hunter, Falconer, Fowler, Fox, Forrester, Archer and Spearman.

The renowned medieval historian Froissart, who eulogised about the romantic deeds of chivalry (and who condemned Scotland as being a poverty stricken wasteland), once sniffily dismissed the peasantry of his native France as the jacquerie (or the jacques-without-names) but it was these same humble folk who ended up overthrowing the arrogant aristocracy.

In the olden days, only the blueblooded knights of antiquity were entitled to full, proper names, both Christian and surnames, but with the passing of time and a more egalitarian, less feudal atmosphere, more respectful and worthy titles spread throughout the populace as a whole.

Echoes of a far distant past can still be found in most names and they can be borne with pride in commemoration of past generations who fought and toiled in some capacity or other to make our nation what it now is, for good or ill.

Chapter two:

Swords and ploughshares

It may be the most common surname throughout the United Kingdom and the USA, but the history and accomplishments of those who have borne the name of Smith are far from commonplace.

From poets and painters to soldiers and statesmen, Smiths have stamped an indelible mark on the world since the name made its first formal appearance in records in the thirteenth and fourteenth centuries.

Its origins stretch much further back in time, however, to those members of tribes and clans who were adept in what were considered the dark mysteries of forging and fashioning metals.

It was a rare and valuable skill, and 'smith' was the occupational name given to these workers in metal.

Knowledge of how to extract metals from ores and then forge and shape them into weapons such as swords, axes, and daggers, was essential for societies engaged in almost constant warfare, while metals also served a crucial function as implements for tilling the ground and harvesting crops.

Precious metals such as gold and silver would be painstakingly and lovingly crafted into gorgeous items of personal decoration and act as status symbols for their proud owners.

Stunningly beautiful examples of early Celtic jewellery still survive, serving as living reminders of the genius of the craftsmen. In later centuries these 'smiths' engaged in the art of crafting jewellery became known as 'gold-smiths.'

From the handling of expensive jew-ellery the art of the 'goldsmith' branched off into the commercial world of trade, and 'gold-smiths' were the forerunners of today's bankers.

The early smiths were also the forerunners of today's scientists, constantly experimenting with methods of mining and extracting ores, smelting them and testing their various qualities.

Many smiths even turned their hands to alchemy – the medieval occult art of seeking the 'elixir of life' and the 'Philosopher's Stone' and transmuting base metals into gold.

This is all a far cry from the popular image of a smith as simply a 'blacksmith', toiling over an anvil with his hammer to make horseshoes!

'Smith' has taken many forms over the centuries, such as Smeayth, Smyth, Smythe, Smyithe, Smijyth, and Smithson (meaning 'son of the smith').

It is a common misconception, however, that the original anglicised version of the name in Scotland, England, and Ireland was 'Smith'.

Old land charters from all three countries reveal the original spelling was Smyth, or Smythe, and became Smith in much the same manner in which the original 'cyder' became the rather more recognisable 'cider'.

Hyphenated versions of the name, such as 'Lindsay – Smith', would be adopted as a means of differentiation from other Smiths or to indicate some other family or clan affiliation.

Smith was also the name adopted by many dispossessed Highland clansmen following the abortive Jacobite Rebellion of 1745, when not only many aspects of an ancient way of life such as the wearing of tartan, the carrying of weapons, and the playing of bagpipes were banned, but also the clan name itself proscribed.

Outlawed as robbers, the MacGregors are an example of a clan forced on some occasions for the sake of survival to adopt a less controversial surname, such as Smith, Grey, or Brown.

In later centuries, many immigrants to the United States found on their arrival at New York's Ellis Island that immigration officials would assign them surnames that were easy to pronounce and spell, such as Smith, as an alternative to what were considered unwieldy and unpronounceable surnames of 'foreign' origin.

Although the name is common throughout both Europe and the United States, however, it is still possible to trace pedigrees back to Scotland, England, or Ireland.

In England, Smythes/Smyths/Smiths flourished for centuries and established identifiable family lineages, particularly on the Isle of Wight, Long Ashton in Somerset, Edmondthorpe in Leicestershire, Great Fenton in Cheshire, and around Nottingham and Mansfield.

In Ireland, noble families bearing the name Smith (later Cusac-Smith) were established in Waterford, Monaghan, Limerick, and Ballygowan, and it is likely that many present-day descendants of Irish immigrants to America could trace a descent back to either of these areas.

The Gaelic version of the surname in

Ireland is MacGowan, or O'Gowan, with the Gaelic word 'ghaba' meaning blacksmith.

Chapter three:

Battle of the clans

It is in Scotland that much of the romance and drama attached to the surname Smith is to be found.

A family of Smythes held Methven Castle, in Perthshire, for a number of centuries, and it was a Thomas Smythe who around 1477 was principal physician to James III. The family crest was a dolphin.

Descendants of these Methven Smythes also acquired the lands of Braco, in Perthshire, with other branches acquiring lands and property as far afield as Stirlingshire, Renfrewshire, Ayrshire, and Aberdeenshire. Smith first appears as a hereditary surname in Aberdeen in 1398.

There were also Smyths of Athernie, in Fife, one of whose illustrious sons was James Carmichael Smyth, physician extraordinary to George III in 1821, while Sir James Smyth fought with distinction under Wellington at Waterloo in 1815.

The Gaelic version of the surname in Scotland is 'Gow', with MacGowan meaning 'son of the Gow', or 'son of the smith.'

The Gows were known as the Slioch Gow Chruim ('the race of the hunch-backed smiths'), and fulfilled a vital role within individual clans as armourers, harness makers, and producers of other essential metallic goods.

The importance of their skill was recognised with the position of 'gow', or 'smith', being held on a hereditary basis.

It was one of these Gows who was responsible for forging an important link with the powerful Clan Chattan, following a curious and bloodthirsty incident that took place on an autumn day on the outskirts of the fair town of Perth back in 1396.

A bitter and bloody feud had endured for centuries between the Clan Kay and the Clan Chattan, a vendetta that not only visited

murder, rape, and pillage on the clans themselves but disrupted the lives of their more
peaceful neighbours.

The monarch, Robert III, decided to
resolve the matter by arranging a gladiatorial
combat involving a fight to the death between
chosen warriors from both clans.

It also provided a rare and exciting
spectacle for the king and the glittering array
of nobles, courtiers, and other associated hang-
ers-on, who witnessed the drama on a large,
flat meadow on the outskirts of Perth known as
the North Inch.

With the young Prince David acting as
umpire and with the eager spectators comfort-
ably seated in specially erected and richly dec-
orated stands, the sixty champions from each
clan were allowed to arm themselves with a
deadly arsenal of swords, dirks, axes, and
crossbows – their only form of protection a
stout leather targe, or shield.

Before the crossbow arrows were
loosed and the clansmen engaged in vicious

hand-to-hand combat, it was discovered that Clan Chattan was a warrior short.

A giant Perth blacksmith known as Henry (or Hal) Gow of the Wynd, however, was allowed to enlist in the ranks of the Chattans to make up the required numbers.

It was a brutal affair. No mercy was accorded to the wounded and no one was allowed to leave the blood-drenched field of combat.

The long afternoon dragged mercilessly on until only Gow and ten Chattan clansmen were left standing. The only surviving Kay champion ran for his life and swam to safety across the River Tay.

As reward for his valiant efforts on behalf of a grateful Clan Chattan, Henry Gow and his family were accorded the honour of being 'adopted' by the Chattans, through the Macphersons, one of the clans that made up what was known as the great confederation of Clan Chattan.

This confederation also included

McGillvrays, McBains, Davidsons, and Farquharsons.

The Macphersons can trace a descent back to Ferchar the Long, a king of Lorne who died in 697, while Clan Chattan held lands in and around the Badenoch region in the Spey Valley.

Followers of St Catain, their crest is a rampant wildcat, and motto 'Touch not the cat without a glove.'

Some authorities assert that Gows, or Smiths, who can trace a descent back to the bold Henry Gow of the Wynd, in Perth, champion of The Battle of the Clans, are entitled to adopt the Chattan crest and motto.

There are at least two Smith tartans. One was designed for Sir William Smith, founder of the Boys' Brigade, while the Gow (Hunting) tartan has been adopted as a Smith tartan.

A charter was granted by the American state of North Carolina in 1978 for a Clan Smith, U.S.A., the chief of whom traces his descent back to an Alfred Smith who was born in the area around Loch Lomond in 1824.

Although not a Highland clan in the traditional sense, Clan Smith nevertheless performs a valuable role in promoting Scottish culture and heritage.

Chapter four:

Wealth of talent

The Smith who has undoubtedly had the greatest impact not only on his native Scotland but also on an international level, is Adam Smith, the son of a customs officer from Kirkcaldy, in Fife.

Born in 1723, he was the author of the landmark *Inquiry into the Nature and Causes of the Wealth of Nations*, an examination of the development of industry and commerce in Europe that helped to lay the foundations of the discipline of economics.

Smith left not only a significant legacy to the modern world, but had an eventful life – not least his kidnapping by gypsies when he was aged four!

Fortunately he was rescued by an uncle and, proving something of a child prodigy, entered the hallowed confines of Glasgow University at the age of only 15, to immerse himself in the study of moral philosophy.

From 1740 until 1746 he studied at Baliol College, Oxford. Returning to Scotland, he was by 1748 delivering popular lectures on the nature, philosophy, and development of wealth, at the same time as becoming acquainted with other great literary, philosophical, and scientific figures such as the philosopher David Hume.

In 1751, aged only 28, Smith was appointed professor of logic at Glasgow University, transferring a year later to the prestigious post of professor of moral philosophy.

A series of lectures on ethics, jurisprudence, rhetoric, and political economy were published in 1759, but Smith resigned from the university four years later to take up the post of tutor to the young Duke of Buccleuch.

This proved to be a significant move, because it allowed Smith to travel widely throughout Europe with his young charge, observing at first hand the operation of the machinery known as capitalism.

He returned to his native Kirkcaldy and put the fruits of his research and observation to work in the production of The Wealth of Nations, which first appeared in 1776. He later settled in Edinburgh, where he died in 1790.

His name is much revered by political economists of the present day, and his book still widely read and quoted by some as the 'Bible' of free trade and capitalism.

It was revealed only after his death that this great exponent of capitalism had used a considerable portion of his own wealth to secretly fund a number of charities.

It is not only in the complex world of economic theory that Smiths have flourished.

John Smith (1747-1807), born at Glenorchy, was a noted Gaelic scholar, while four Smiths were renowned portrait painters: Charles Smith (1749-1824), was a native of Orkney and friend of the English painter Sir Joshua Reynolds, while Colvin Smith, born in 1795, and whose father hailed from Brechin, was a member of the Royal Scottish Academy and executed a noted portrait of the great novelist Sir Walter Scott.

Colvin Smith traced a descent from Smiths who were hereditary armourers to the Bishops of Brechin.

Two great English portrait painters were John Raphael Smith (1752-1812), from Derby, and William Smith of Chichester (1707-64).

In the world of military affairs, Thomas Smith, executed as a traitor in 1708, was a colourful adventurer who, after holding various commands in the Royal Navy and having been court-martialled and dismissed from service, entered the service of the French.

He was instrumental in the capture of an English vessel off Harwich, and, taking command of the ship, boldly attempted to capture Harwich itself!

Needless to say, the attempt failed, and Smith was captured and suffered the dire penalty of being hanged, drawn, and quartered.

Thomas Smith (1600-27) was a soldier

from Berwick-on-Tweed, who in the course of his short life wrote military works, including *The Art of Gunnery*, that remained in use for a number of centuries.

The Baptist religious sect that flourishes today owes its early origins to the Englishman John Smyth, who died in 1612, while Joseph Smith (1805-44) was the American founder of the Mormons.

William Robertson Smith (1846-94) was a Scottish biblical scholar whose contribution on the Bible for the 9th edition of the *Encyclopaedia Britannica* led to an unsuccessful prosecution for heresy, while Sydney Smith (1771-1845), was an Anglican divine who supported Catholic emancipation and founded the *Edinburgh Review*.

Scots-born Sir William Alexander Smith (1854-1914), was the founder in 1883 of the Boy's Brigade movement, while John Smith (1580-1631) was a daring English adventurer who famously had his life saved by Pocahontas while on a colonising expedition to Virginia.

In the world of music, one of the most famous of the Gows was Neil Gow, who was born at Inver, near Dunkeld, in 1727.

Taking up the violin, or fiddle, at the tender age of nine, Gow's foot-tapping strathspeys and reels gained him the renowned title of 'The Prince of Fiddlers.'

In more recent times, the British Labour Party recognises Scots-born John Smith as one of its greatest leaders.

An ardent supporter of devolution for Scotland, Smith trained as a barrister and entered Parliament in 1970 as Labour member for North Lanarkshire.

Widely expected to lead his party to power, his untimely death came in 1994, at the age of 55.

He was buried on the island of Iona and there is a memorial to him at the magnificent new Scottish Parliament building in Edinburgh.

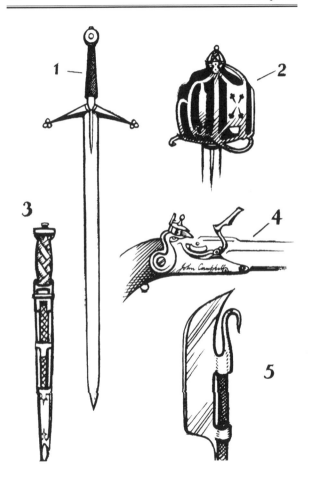

Clan weapons

1) The claymore or two-handed sword
   (fifteenth or early sixteenth century)

2) Basket hilt of broadsword
   made in Stirling, 1716

3) Highland dirk
   (eighteenth century)

4) Steel pistol *(detail)* made in Doune

5) Head of Lochaber Axe as carried
   in the '45 and earlier